Contents

Selecting Fabrics

Fabric is usually selected after a quilt design and color scheme have been chosen, although a special piece of fabric may help create a design idea or establish color for a quilt. Many kinds of fabric can be used for a quilt, but a primary consideration is fiber content.

Fabric of 100 percent cotton is the best choice for quilts. Cotton fabric is easy to cut, sew, and mark; it is also easy to press, holds a crease well, and is available in a wide range of colors and prints. The quality and weight of cotton fabric is determined by thread count. The thread count is the number of threads per inch (2.5 cm) of fabric. In high-quality cotton fabric, the thread count is equal lengthwise and crosswise; this is called an even weave. Most quilting cottons are either 78-square or 68-square. Fabrics with lower thread counts are too lightweight.

Cotton/polyester blends resist wrinkling and abrasion, making them a suitable choice for frequently washed quilts. The different lengthwise and crosswise thread counts in cotton/polyester blends cause a different amount of stretch along the lengthwise and crosswise grains, which can make it more difficult to piece fabrics accurately. Also, when stitched, cotton/polyester blends tend to pucker more than 100 percent cotton fabrics.

Choose good-quality fabrics that are compatible with the function of your quilt. If you are making a comforter for a child's bed, the quilt will be subject to hard and constant use; select fabrics that can withstand wear and frequent washing. If you are making a wall hanging, the durability of the fabric is less important.

Types of Quilting Fabrics

Quilting fabrics include prints, tone-on-tones, solids, broadcloths, hand-dyed fabrics, flannels, backing fabrics, and muslin.

Prints can include calicos, country prints, novelty prints, and designer-inspired prints. Tone-on-tones are used for backgrounds and transitions in your quilt design.

Solids and broadcloths come in every color including black and white. Kona brand is readily available.

Hand-dyed fabrics are 100 percent cotton and are available in gradations of color and other designs. Hand-dyed fabrics give your quilt a unique look. These fabrics can be purchased at some quilting stores, quilting shows, and from mail-order sources.

Flannel suitable for quilting is available at some quilt stores. It is especially nice for children's quilts. It also makes a cozy backing for your quilt.

Muslin is a utility fabric used for foundation bases. It is generally a lighter weave and comes in a variety of widths.

Selecting Batting

Batting is the middle layer of a quilt. The loft, or thickness, of the batting determines the warmth or springiness of the quilt. Batting is purchased according to the amount of loft desired (opposite). The most widely used fibers for batting are cotton and polyester, or a blend of the two (referred to as 80/20). Cotton batting gives a flat, traditional appearance when quilted. Polyester batting gives a puffy look and is more stable and easier to handle than cotton batting. Cotton/polyester batting combines the flat appearance of cotton with the stability and ease in handling of polyester. New fiber blends are now available including bamboo and silk. Fusible batting eliminates the need for hand basting. It is useful for smaller lap quilts. Your quilt shop can advise you on the benefits of each type of batting.

Two types of batting are frequently used: bonded and needlepunch. Bonded batting is made by layering fibers and then adding a finish to hold the fibers together and make the batting easier to handle. Needlepunch batting is made by layering the fibers and then passing them through a needling machine to give a dense, low-loft batting. It is firm, easy to handle, and warm. Most needlepunch batting is polyester. The minimum distance between quilting stitches varies from one batting type to another and is noted on the batting package.

The fibers in batting may migrate, or move, affecting the appearance of the quilt. Bonded batting is treated to help control fiber migration. There are two forms of fiber migration: bunching and bearding. Bunching is the migration of fibers within a quilt, causing thick and thin areas. Bunching can be controlled by placing the quilting stitches ½" to 1" (1.3 to 2.5 cm) apart. Bearding is the migration of fibers through the surface of the quilt. Polyester batting tends to beard, and these fibers may pill. Cotton batting may beard, but the fibers break off at the surface. To help prevent bearding, use a closely woven fabric for the quilt top and backing. Black batting is the best choice for a dark colored quilt. If bearding does occur, clip the fibers close to the surface of the quilt: do not pull the batting through the fabric. After clipping the fibers, pull the quilt top away from the batting so the fibers return to the inside of the quilt.

Batting is available in a wide range of sizes, although the selection in certain fibers and construction types may be limited. Polyester batting has the widest range of sizes and lofts. Batting should extend 2" to 4" (5 to 10 cm) beyond the edges of the quilt top on all sides to allow for the shrinkage that occurs during quilting. Batting is packaged for standard-size quilts. It is also available by the yard and in smaller packages for clothing and craft projects.

Guidelines for Selecting Batting

Fiber Content	Appearance of Finished Quilt	Characteristics	Spacing of Quilting Stitches
Cotton	Flat	Absorbs moisture, cool in summer and warm in winter	½" to 1" (1.3 to 2.5 cm)
Polyester	Puffy	Warmth and loft without weight, nonallergenic, moth and mildew-resistant	3" to 5" (7.5 to 12.5 cm)
Cotton/polyester blend	Moderately flat	Combines characteristics of cotton and polyester	2" to 4" (5 to 10 cm)

Batting Thickness

Low-loft	⅛" to ⅜" (3 mm to 1cm)
Medium-loft	½" to ¾" (1.3 to 2 cm)
High-loft	1" to 2" (2.5 to 5 cm)
Extra-high-loft	2" to 3" (5 to 7.5 cm)

Packaged Batting Sizes

Crib	45"x 60" (115 x 152.5 cm)
Twin	72"x 90" (183 x 229 cm)
Full	81"x 96" (206 x 244 cm)
Queen	90"x 108" (229 x 274.5 cm)
King	120"x 120" (305 x 305 cm)

Tips for Selecting Batting

Low-loft bonded cotton or cotton/polyester batting is easiest to handle.

Medium-loft adds texture to the finished quilt. The higher the loft, the more difficult to machine-quilt.

High-loft and extra-high-loft battings are best used for tied quilts because they are difficult to machine-quilt.

Notions and Equipment

A few carefully selected notions can make quilting easier and help improve your accuracy in cutting, marking, and sewing.

Quilting can be done entirely on a straight-stitch conventional sewing machine. Choosing the correct type of sewing machine accessories, such as presser feet and needle plates, can help improve your results.

Measuring & Cutting Tools

See-through rulers (1) serve as both a measuring tool and a straightedge for cutting with a rotary cutter.

Measurements are visible through the ruler, so you can cut without marking. Many sizes and types of see-through rulers are available. A ruler 6"× 24" (15 × 61 cm) is recommended, because it is versatile.

Features of rulers vary widely. Some rulers are printed with measurements in two colors to show clearly on both light and dark fabrics. Some have a lip on one edge to hook onto the edge of the cutting mat for easier alignment. Some are printed on the underside to prevent distortion and increase accuracy; if the lines and numbers are molded on the underside, it will help prevent slippage. Square rulers, and rulers with 30°, 45°,

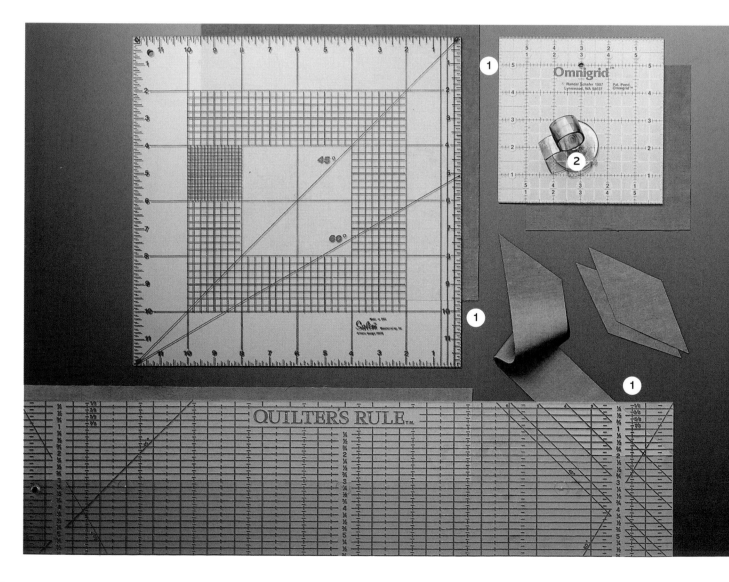

and 60° angle lines, are available. Choose rulers that have the features most important for the type of quilting you are planning to do.

Suction rings (2) and **suction handles** (3) are available to help in positioning a ruler.

Rotary cutters (4) allow you to cut smooth edges on multiple layers of fabric quickly and easily. The cutters are available in various sizes: the smaller size works well for cutting curves or a few layers of fabric; the larger sizes work well for cutting long, straight edges or many layers of fabric.

Cutting mats (5), made especially for use with rotary cutters, protect the blades and the table. They may be plain, or printed with a grid and diagonal lines. A mat printed with a grid is helpful for cutting right angles. Mats come in a variety of sizes. Choose a mat at least 22" (56 cm) wide to accommodate a width of fabric folded in half.

Sewing scissors (6) and **shears** (7) are used for cutting shapes and clipping threads. **Craft knives** (8) are used for cutting cardboard, paper, and plastic templates for pieced or appliquéd designs.

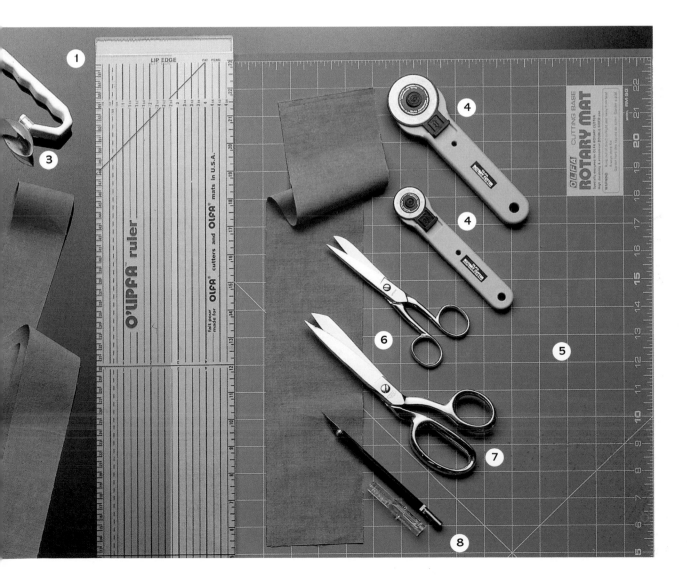

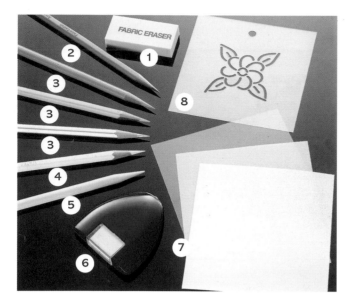

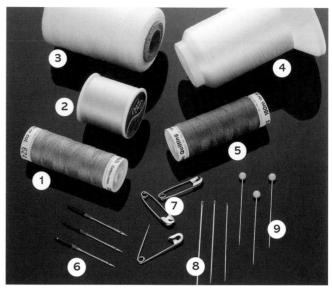

Marking Tools

The markings on a quilt should last only as long as you need them, and you should be able to remove them easily and thoroughly without damaging the quilt. Always test markers on fabrics to see how long the markings last and to be sure they can be removed. Mark lightly; it is more difficult to remove markings that are embedded in the fibers.

A special **fabric eraser** (1) can be used to remove **light lead pencil** (2) marks without abrading or leaving marks on the fabric. **Oil-free and wax-free colored pencils** (3) may also be used for marking. Choose a color close to the fabric color; or choose silver, because it shows on most fabrics. Remove marks before pressing the fabric or washing it in hot water; heat may set pencil marks. **White water-soluble pencils** (4) are available for marking dark fabrics; remove marks with a damp cloth. **Soapstone pencils** (5) are made of pressed talc and marks can be rubbed off or wiped off with water.

Chalk wheels (6) are available in a variety of shapes and colors; marking id fine and accurate. Chalk-wheel marks brush off easily, are washable, and will not stain.

A variety of **plastic sheets** (7) is available for making your own templates. **Precut templates** (8) are available for marking traditional quilting designs.

Sewing & Quilting Tools

For ease in stitching, thread should be of good quality. For piecing, use **100 percent cotton** (1) or **all-purpose sewing thread** (2); match thread color to the darker fabric or use a neutral color, such as black, cream or gray, to blend. For basting, use a fine, **white cotton basting thread** (3), or white all-purpose thread; the dye from dark thread could rub off on fabrics.

For quilting, 100 percent cotton thread is usually the best choice. Fine, .004 mm, or size 80 **monofilament nylon thread** (4), which comes in smoke or clear, is good for quilting and for invisibly stitching appliqués, because it blends with all colors. **Cotton quilting thread** (5) without a finish may be used for machine quilting; however, quilting thread with a special glace finish should not be used for machine quilting. Quilting thread may either match or contrast with the fabric.

Insert a new **sewing machine needle** (6) before beginning a quilting project. For piecing and appliqué, use a size 9/70 or 11/80; for machine quilting, use a size 11/80 or 14/90 needle, depending on the thickness and fiber content of the batting.

Safety pins (7) are essential for pin-basting a quilt; 1" (2.5 cm) rustproof pins work well for most quilting projects. Use **milliners' needles** (8) for thread-basting, because they are long and have small, round eyes. Use glass-head **quilting pins** (9), because they are long, 1¾" (4.5 cm), and strong.

Sewing Machine Equipment

A straight-stitch conventional sewing machine is used for quilting. The stitch length should be easy to adjust, because you start and end lines of stitches by gradually increasing or decreasing the stitch length.

An entire quilt can be made using only the straight stitch, but several additional features, common on most sewing machines, expand your quilting options. A blind-hem stitch can be used for attaching appliqués. Feed dogs that can be covered or dropped allow you to do freehand quilting.

Presser Feet

Special presser feet are not necessary foe machine quilting, but they can improve your results. For machine-guided quilting, an **Even Feed foot** (1) is recommended for pucker-free stitching. The feed dogs on the Even Feed foot work with the feed dogs of the sewing machine to pull layers of fabric through at the same rate of speed. For freehand quilting, you can either use a **darning foot** (2) or stitch without a foot, depending on the sewing machine.

Use a **general-purpose foot** (3), or a special-purpose foot for zigzag and blindstitching. A **straight-stitch foot** (4) can improve the quality of stitches, particularly when piecing fabrics with the narrow seam allowances that are standard in quilting.

Needle Plates

Use a **general-purpose needle plate** (5) with the general-purpose or special-purpose foot for zigzag and blindstitching. Use a **straight-stitch needle plate** (6) with the straight-stitch foot for straight and uniform seams and quilting lines. The small hole in the needle plate keeps the fabric from being pushed down into the sewing machine as you stitch. Also use the straight-stitch needle plate with the Even Feed foot for machine-guided quilting and with the darning foot for freehand quilting.

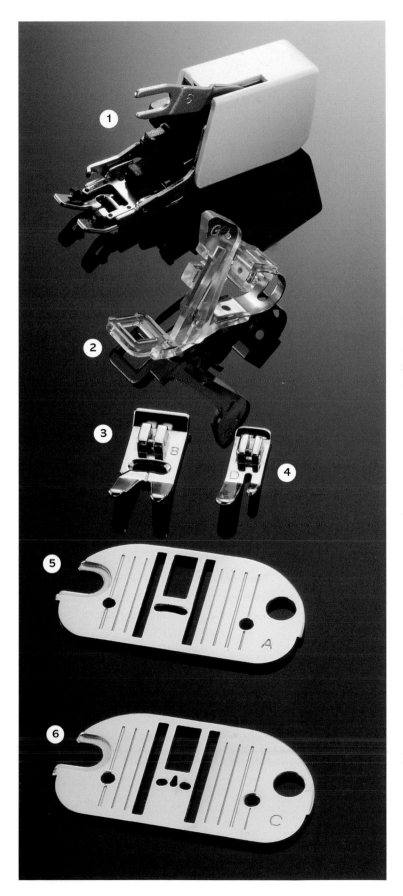

Techniques

Cutting

The quick-cutting techniques that follow are both timesaving and accurate. Instead of cutting each piece of the quilt individually, stack several layers of fabric and cut them into crosswise strips. The pieces are then cut from these strips, eliminating the need for templates.

Determine the grainline by folding the fabric in half and holding it by the selvages. Then shift one side until the fabric hangs straight. It is not necessary to straighten quilting fabrics that are off-grain or to pull threads or tear fabrics to find the grainline.

Good-quality cutting equipment helps ensure that every piece you cut is exactly the right size and that all the pieces fit together perfectly. Use a rotary cutter with a sharp blade and a cutting mat with a printed grid.

Tape three or four thin strips of fine sandpaper across the width of the bottom of a see-through ruler, using double-stick tape. This prevents the ruler from slipping when you are cutting fabric.

How to Cut Fabric Strips

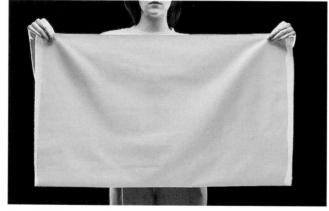

1 Fold fabric in half, selvages together. Hold selvage edges, letting fold hang free. Shift one side of fabric until fold hangs straight. Fold line is straight of grain.

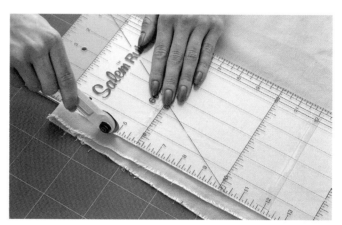

2 Lay fabric on cutting mat, with fold along a grid line. Place ruler on fabric close to raw edge at 90° angle to fold. Trim along edge of ruler. Hold ruler firmly; apply steady, firm pressure on blade. Stop when rotary cutter gets past hand.

3 Leave blade in position; reposition hand ahead of blade. Hold firmly and continue cutting. Make sure the fabric and ruler do not shift position.

4 Place ruler on fabric, aligning trimmed edge with desired measurement. Hold ruler firmly; cut as in steps 2 and 3. After cutting several strips, check fabric to be sure it is still on-grain.

Stitching

For pieced quilts, seam allowances are traditionally ¼" (6 mm); stitch accurate seam allowances, so all pieces will fit together exactly. If you have a seam guide on your sewing machine, check the placement of the ¼" (6 mm) mark by stitching on a scrap of fabric. If your machine does not have a seam guide, mark one on the bed of the machine with tape.

Use a stitch length of about 15 stitches per inch (2.5 cm). A shorter stitch length may be necessary for stitching curves and is used for securing stitches at the ends of seams. Adjust thread tensions evenly, so the fabric does not pucker when stitched.

Chainstitching is a timesaving technique for piecing. Seams are stitched without stopping and cutting the threads between them. After all the pieces are stitched together, the connecting threads are clipped and the seams are finger-pressed.

Although some quilters prefer working on one block at a time for the satisfaction of completing a block quickly, it is more efficient to sew an entire quilt top in units. Chainstitch together all the smallest pieces from all the blocks; then combine them to create larger units.

How to Chain and Assemble Pieces

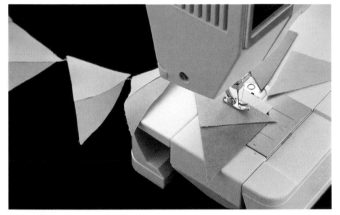

1 Start with smallest pieces; stitch together without backstitching or stopping between pieces, to make a chain of two-piece units. Clip threads between units; finger-press seams.

2 Add more pieces to unit, if necessary for quilt block design, chainstitching them together. Clip threads and finger-press.

3 Chainstitch units together to create larger units. Clip threads and finger-press.

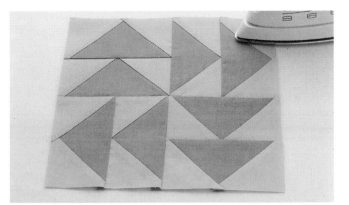

4 Stitch larger units together to form quilt block. Press with iron.

Pressing

Seams are usually pressed to one side in quilts; however, if you are planning to do stipple quilting you may prefer to press the seams open to make it easier to quilt. When pressing seams to one side, it is best to press them to the darker fabric to prevent show-through.

Do not press seams with an iron until a unit or block has straight of grain on all four sides. Always remove all markings from the fabrics before pressing, because the heat from the iron may set marks permanently. When pressing seams, use steam rather than pressure, to prevent the layers from imprinting on the right side. A heavy pressing motion can distort the shape and size of the pieces. Press the blocks first from the wrong side; then press them again lightly from the right side.

The quilt should not be pressed after it is completed because pressing will flatten the batting.

Tips for Pressing

Finger-press individual seam allowances; pressing with an iron can distort bias seams. Press with iron only after a unit or block has straight of grain on all four sides.

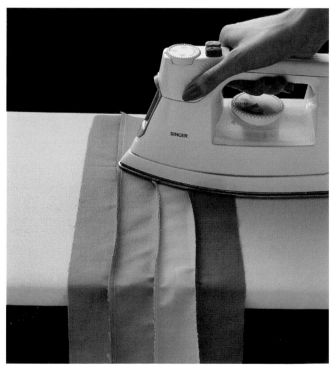

Press long seams with iron by placing strips across, rather than lengthwise on, ironing board, to prevent distorting grainline as you press.

Sashing

Sashing strips frame individual quilt blocks and unify the entire quilt top. Sashing strips also change the finished size of a quilt. You can make a larger quilt from a small number of quilt blocks by adding sashing strips.

Plain sashing is a good choice for a quilt with a complex block design. Sashing with connecting squares adds more interest to a quilt. Use pieced connecting squares when the block design is less complex. The square can be any pieced design, such as a small nine-patch quilt block.

To determine the number of sashing strips required, refer to a sketch of the quilt top.

Specific measurements are not given in the instructions that follow, because the measurements are determined by the size of the blocks and the desired finished size of the quilt.

How to Make Plain Sashing Strips

1 Cut strips (page 10) to width specified in project directions. Or cut strips to desired width of sashing plus ½" (1.3 cm) for seam allowances.

2 Measure all sides of several quilt blocks to determine the shortest measurement; cut short sashing strips to this length.

3 Stitch short sashing strips between blocks, right sides together, to form rows; do not stitch strips to ends of rows. Press seam allowances toward sashing.

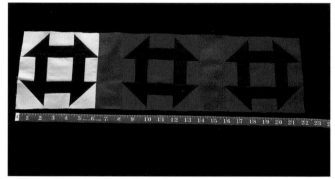

4 Measure length of rows to determine shortest measurement. Cut long sashing strips to this length, piecing as necessary.

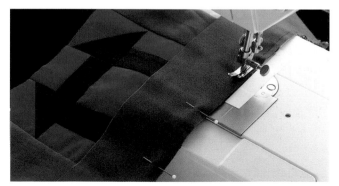

5 Mark centers of sashing strips and rows. Place one long sashing strip along bottom of one row of blocks, right sides together; match and pin centers and ends. Pin along length, easing in any excess fullness; stitch. Repeat for remaining rows, except for bottom row.

6 Align rows of blocks and mark sashing strips, as shown. Pin bottom of sashing strip to top of next row, right sides together; align marks to seamlines. Stitch as in step 5. Press seam allowances toward sashing. Continue until all rows are attached.

How to Make Sashing Strips with Connecting Squares

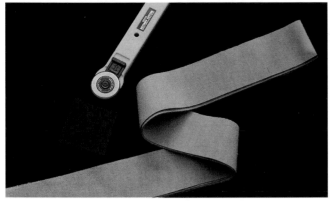

1 Cut strips (page 10) to width specified in project directions. Or cut strips to desired width of sashing plus ½" (1.3 cm) for seam allowances. Cut squares for corners from contrasting fabric the width of sashing strip.

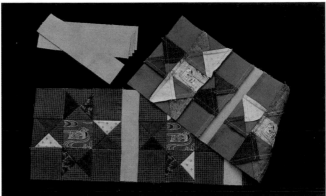

2 Measure all sides of several blocks to determine shortest measurement; cut sashing strips this length. Stitch strips between blocks, right sides together, to form rows; ease in fullness. Do not stitch strips to ends of rows. Press seam allowances toward strips.

3 Stitch the remaining sashing strips alternately to sashing squares, to equal length of block and sashing row. Press seam allowances toward sashing strips.

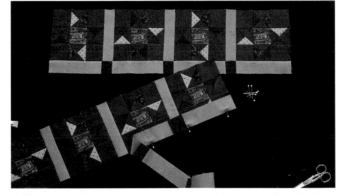

4 Place sashing unit along bottom of first row of blocks, right sides together, matching seams. Pin along length, easing in any fullness; stitch. Repeat for remaining rows, except for bottom row.

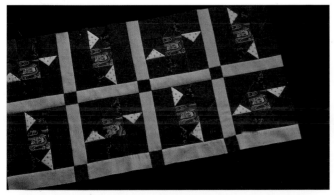

5 Pin bottom of one long sashing strip to top of next row, matching seams, as in step 4; stitch. Press seam allowances toward sashing strip. Continue until all rows are attached.

Alternate design. Make connecting checkerboard squares. Choose a width for sashing and finished squares that can be easily divided by 3.

Borders and Corners

Border strips can be cut on the crosswise or lengthwise grain of the fabric. Cutting them on the crosswise grain may save on the amount of fabric needed, but may require that the strips be pieced to make up the necessary length.

If the strips need to be pieced, the seams may be stitched either straight across the width of the strips, or diagonally on the bias; they may be placed in the center of the border. Seams can be concealed better in a printed fabric then in a solid-color fabric.

There are several ways to stitch corners of a border. The lapped corner is the simplest method. Mitered corners are frequently used for striped or border-print fabrics. Interrupted borders have a contrasting block at each corner, such as a nine-patch block.

Multiple borders are frequently used to incorporate more than one color from the quilt top. After the first border is stitched, the second border is added, using the same method. If lapped corners are used, they are lapped in the same direction on both borders.

How to Make a Lapped Corner

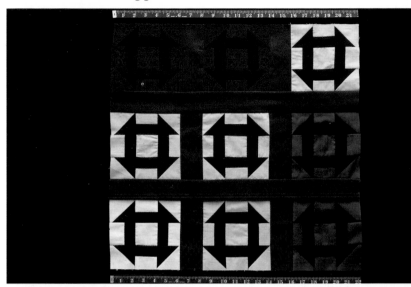

1 Measure top and bottom rows of quilt top. Cut two strips, with length of strips equal to shorter measurement, piecing as necessary; width of strips is equal to finished width of border plus ½" (1.3 cm).

2 Pin strip to upper edge of quilt top, right sides together, at center and at two ends; pin along length, easing in any fullness. Stitch; press seam allowance toward border. Repeat at lower edge.

3 Measure sides of the quilt top, including border strips. Cut two strips as in step 1. Pin and stitch to sides of quilt top as in step 2, including top and bottom border strips in seams.

How to Make a Border with Mitered Corners

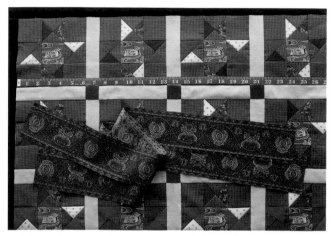

1 Measure top and bottom rows of the quilt top to determine shorter measurement. Cut two strips, with length equal to shorter measurement plus 2 times finished width of border plus 1" (2.5 cm), and width equal to finished width of border plus ½" (1.3 cm)

2 Mark center of top and bottom rows and center of each border strip. From each end of border strip, mark the finished width of the border plus ½" (1.3 cm). Match center of one border strip to center of top edge of quilt top, right sides together; pin.

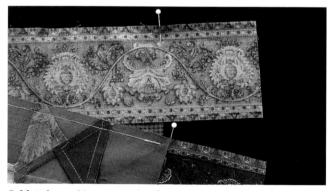

3 Match markings at ends of strip to edges of quilt top; pin. Continue pinning along edge, easing in any fullness. Stitch, beginning and ending ¼" (6 mm) from edges of quilt top; backstitch at ends. Repeat for bottom edge of quilt top.

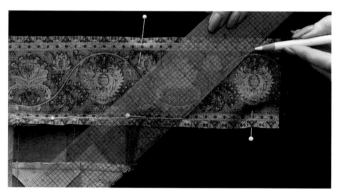

4 Repeat steps 1, 2 and 3 for sides or quilt top. Fold quilt top diagonally, right sides together, matching seamlines; pin securely. Draw diagonal line on border strip, extending line formed by fold or quilt top.

5 Stitch on marked line; do not catch seam allowances in stitching. Trim ends of border strips to ¼" (6 mm) seam allowances.

6 Press seam allowances open at corner; press remaining seam allowances toward border strip. Repeat for remaining corners.

How to Make a Border with Interrupted Corners

1 Measure top and bottom rows of the quilt top to determine the shorter measurement. Cut four strips of Fabric A and eight strips of Fabric B, with length equal to shorter measurement and width equal to one-third the finished width of border plus ½" (1.3 cm). Measure sides of quilt and cut strips.

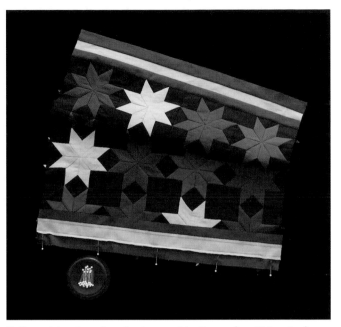

2 Sew strips together for top and bottom of quilt top to form two B-A-B units. Pin one pieced border to top of quilt, right sides together, at center and two ends; pin along length, easing in any fullness. Stitch. Press seam allowance toward border. Repeat with remaining unit at bottom.

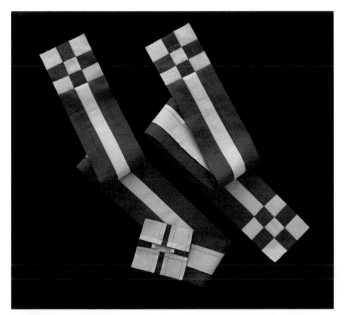

3 Sew strips together for sides to form two B-A-B units. Make four 9-patch blocks, using same width measurements as in step 1, above. Stitch one block to each end of border strips. Press seam allowances toward borders.

4 Pin and stitch the borders to sides of quilt, as in step 2, above, matching seams at corners. Press seam allowances toward border.

Marking

Quilting designs should be marked on the quilt top, unless the design follows the piecing or appliqué lines, as in echo or outline quilting.

Test the marking tools on the fabrics in the quilt top before marking. Be sure the marks can withstand handling, folding, and rolling, and that they can be thoroughly brushed, erased, or washed away after quilting.

It is easier to mark the quilt top before the layers are basted together. Place the quilt top on a hard, flat surface and draw or trace the design accurately with a clear, thin line.

If you are using a template to mark the design on a border, mark the corners first. If a design of repeating motifs does not fit, adjust the length of several motifs as necessary. You can use a single motif at the corners of the border or mark intersecting lines of channel quilting (page 27) to form a grid.

Guides used for making quilting lines are rulers and plastic templates.

How to Mark a Quilting Design

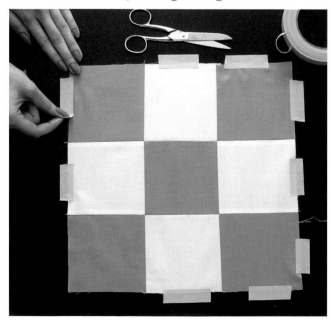

1 Press quilt top; place on hard, flat work surface, with corners square and sides parallel. Tape securely, keeping quilt top smooth and taut.

2 Mark quilting design, using ruler or template as a guide, beginning in corners. Mark distinct, thin lines, using as light a touch as possible.

Batting and Backing

Although batting is available in different sizes, it may need to be pieced for larger projects. Battings differ in loft and fiber content (pages 4 and 5). Loft is the thickness and springiness of a batting. It determines the degree of texture in a quilt.

The batting and backing should extend 2" to 4" (5 to 10 cm) beyond the edges of the quilt top on all sides, to allow for the shrinkage that occurs during quilting. It may be necessary to piece the batting and backing.

How to Piece Batting and Backing Fabric

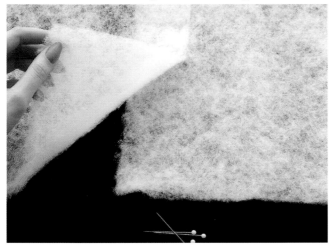

1 Batting. Overlap two pieces of batting, 1" to 2" (2.5 to 5 cm).

2 Cut with shears through both layers, down the center of overlapped section.

3 Remove trimmed edges. Butt batting edges, and whipstitch by hand to secure.

Backing Cut selvages from fabric. Piece fabric as necessary. Stitch, using a stitch length of 12 to 15 stitches per inch (2.5 cm) and ¼" (6 mm) seam allowances. Press seam allowances to one side or open.

Basting the Layers

Basting keeps the three layers of the quilt from shifting during the quilting process. Traditionally, quilts were basted using needle and thread; however, safety-pin basting may be used instead.

Lay the quilt out flat on a hard surface, such as the floor or a large table and baste the entire quilt. Or baste the quilt in sections on a table at least one-fourth the size of the quilt.

Press the quilt top and backing fabric flat before layering and basting. If basting with safety pins, use 1" (2.5 cm) rustproof steel pins. Steel pins glide through fabrics more easily than brass pins, and the 1" (2.5 cm) size is easier to handle.

If basting with thread, use white cotton thread and a large milliners' or darning needle. Use a large running stitch, about 1" (2.5 cm) long. Pull the stitches snug so the layers will not shift. Backstitch at the ends to secure the stitching.

How to Baste a Quilt

1 Fold quilt top, right sides together, into quarters, without creasing. Mark center of each side at raw edges with safety pins. Repeat for batting and backing, folding backing wrong sides together.

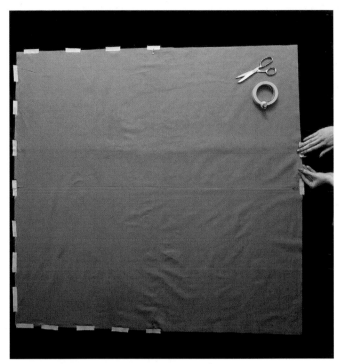

2 Unfold backing on work surface, wrong side up. Tape securely, beginning at center of each side and working toward corners, stretching fabric slightly. Backing should be taut, but not overly stretched.

3 Place batting on backing, matching pins on each side. Smooth, but do not stretch, working from center of quilt out to sides.

4 Place quilt top, right side up, on batting, matching pins on each side; smooth, but do not stretch.

How to Baste a Quilt (cont.)

5 Baste with pins or thread from center of quilt to pins on sides; if thread-basting, pull stitches snug so layers will not shift. Avoid basting on marked quilting lines or through seams.

6 Baste one quarter section in parallel rows about 6" (15 cm) apart, working toward raw edges. If thread-basting, also baste quarter-section in parallel rows in opposite direction.

7 Repeat step 6 for remaining quarter sections. Remove tape from backing.

8 Fold edges of backing over batting and edges of quilt top to prevent raw edges of fabric from raveling and batting from catching on needle and feed dogs during quilting. Pin-baste.

Machine Quilting Basics

When machine-quilting, it is necessary to roll or fold the quilt in order for it to fit under the sewing machine head and to prevent it from hanging over the edge of the table. You may want to expand your sewing surface to support the quilt.

Always keep the largest section of quilt to the left of the needle as you stitch. As you quilt from the center toward the sides, there is less fabric to feed under the head of the machine, making the quilt easier to manage.

Cotton or monofilament nylon thread may be used for quilting (page 8). If using monofilament nylon thread, use it only in the needle and use a thread that matches the backing fabric in the bobbin. Loosen the needle thread tension so the bobbin thread does not show on the right side.

When machine quilting, stitch continuously, minimizing starts and stops as much as possible. Check for any tucks in the backing by feeling through the layers of the quilt ahead of the sewing machine needle. Prevent the tucks from being stitched by continuously easing in the excess fabric before it reaches the needle. If a tuck does occur, release stitches for 3" (7.5 cm) or more, and restitch, easing in excess fabric.

Quilting Techniques

For machine-guided quilting, such as stitch-in-the-ditch and channel quilting, it is helpful to stitch with an Even Feed foot, or walking foot (1), if one is available; this type of presser foot helps to prevent puckering. Position your hands on either side of the presser foot and hold the fabric taut to prevent the layers from shifting. Stitch, using a stitch length of 10 to 12 stitches per inch (2.5 cm), and ease any excess fabric under the foot as you stitch. The presser foot and feed dogs guide the quilt through the machine.

For free-motion quilting, such as template, motif, and stipple quilting, remove the regular presser foot and attach a darning foot (2). Set the machine for a straight stitch, and use a straight-stitch needle plate; cover the feed dogs, or lower them. It is not necessary to adjust the stitch length setting on the machine, because the stitch length is determined by a combination of the movement of the quilt and the speed of the needle. Use your hands to guide the fabric as you stitch, applying gentle tension. With the presser foot lifter in the lowered position, stitch, moving the fabric with wrist and hand movements. Maintain a steady rhythm and speed as you stitch, to keep the stitch length uniform. When changing your hand positions, stop stitching, with the needle down in the fabric.

Quilting Sequence

Plan the stitching sequence before you begin to quilt. First quilt the longest or largest sections, working from the center toward the sides. For example, for a quilt with sashing, quilt the sashing strips before quilting the blocks, starting with the center strips and working toward the side strips. This helps anchor the layers throughout the quilt to prevent them from shifting.

Next, quilt the areas within the blocks that will not be heavily quilted, such as motifs. Then proceed to the smaller areas or those that will be more heavily quilted.

The sequence for quilting varies with the style of the quilt. For quilts with side-by-side blocks, anchor the layers throughout the quilt by stitching in the ditch between the blocks in vertical and horizontal rows. For a medallion quilt, stitch in the ditch along the border seam to anchor the layers; then quilt the central area.

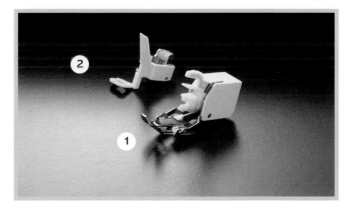

How to Secure the Thread Tails

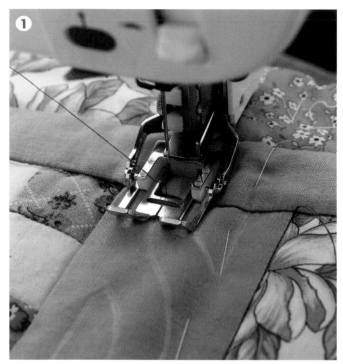

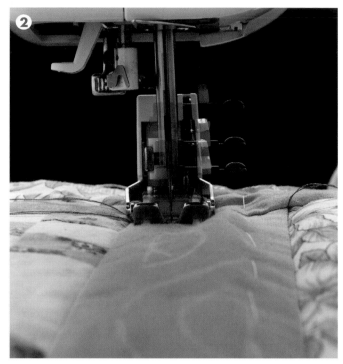

1. Draw up the bobbin thread to the quilt top by turning flywheel by hand and stopping with needle at highest position. Pull on needle thread to bring the bobbin thread up through the fabric.

2. Stitch several short stitches to secure threads at the beginning of stitching line, gradually increasing stitch length for about ½" (1.3 cm), until it is desired length. Reverse procedure at end of stitching.

How to Quilt Using Machine-guided and Free-motion Techniques

Stitch-in-the-ditch quilting. Stitch over the seamline, stitching in the well of the seam.

Channel quilting. Stitch parallel quilting lines, starting with inner marked line and working outward.

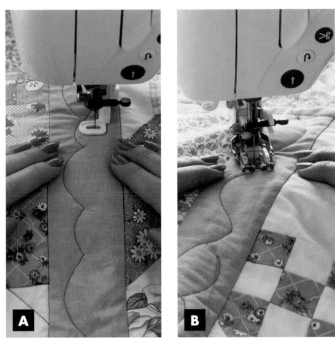

Single-motif template quilting with plastic stencils. Mark design, using marking pencil and plastic stenci. Stitch as much of design as possible in long, continuous lines, without stopping.

Continuous-motif template quilting with plastic stencils. Mark design, using marking pencil and stencil. Stitch motifs along one side to points where motifs connect (A). Or stitch one side of first motif, then opposite side of second motif, and repeat (B). Return to starting point; stitch motifs on opposite side.

Template quilting with tear-away stencils. Stitch either single motif or continuous motif, following the directional arrows on paper stencil. Tear away the paper stencil.

Stipple quilting. Stitch random, curving lines, beginning and ending at an edge and covering background evenly. Work in small sections; keep spaces between quilting lines close. Do not cross over lines.

Motif quilting. Determine longest continuous stitching line possible around desired motif. Stitch around motif without stopping; continue to next motif. Stitch any additional design lines as necessary.

Binding

How to Bind a Quilt with Double Lapped Binding

1 Fold fabric in half on lengthwise grainline. Cut strips 3" (7.5 cm) on crosswise grainline.

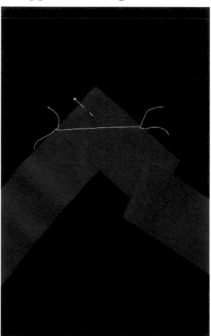

2 Pin strips, right sides together, at right angles; strips will form a V. Stitch diagonally across strips.

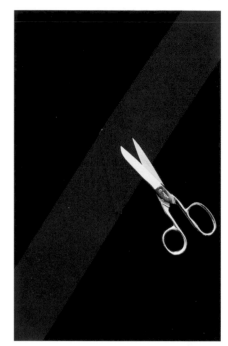

3. Trim the seam allowances to ¼" (6 mm). Press seam open. Trim points even with edges.

4 Measure one side of quilt; cut binding this length plus 2" (5 cm). Mark binding 1" (2.5 cm) in from each end; divide section between pins in quarters; pin-mark. Divide sides of quilt in quarters; pin-mark.

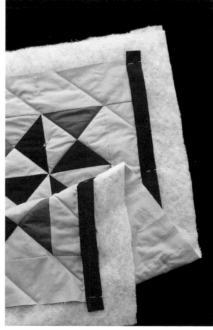

5 Fold binding in half lengthwise, wrong sides together. Place binding on quilt top, matching raw edges and pin-marks; binding will extend 1" (2.5 cm) beyond quilt top at each end.

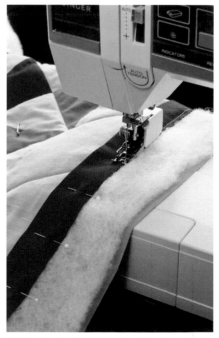

6 Stitch binding to quilt ¼" (6 mm) from raw edges of binding.

How to Bind a Quilt with Double Lapped Binding (cont.)

7 Cut excess batting and backing to ½" (1.3 cm) from stitching line.

8 Wrap binding around edge of quilt, covering stitching line on back of quilt; pin.

9 Stitch in the ditch on the right side of quilt, catching binding on back of quilt.

10 Repeat steps 4 to 9 for opposite side of quilt. Trim ends of binding even with edges of quilt top.

11 Repeat steps 4 to 7 for remaining two sides. Trim ends of binding to extend ½" (1.3 cm) beyond finished edges of quilt.

12 Fold binding down along the stitching line. Fold ½" (1.3 cm) end of binding over finished edge; press in place. Wrap binding around edge and stitch in the ditch as in steps 8 and 9. Slipstitch end by hand.

How to Bind a Quilt with Double Mitered Binding

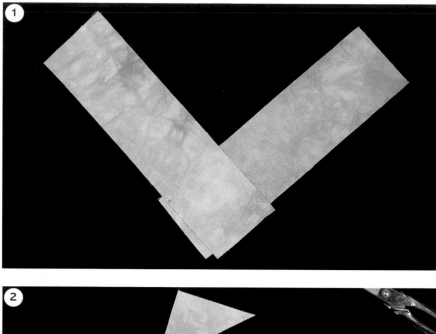

1 Trim the batting and backing even with the edges of the quilt top. Measure perimeter of quilt; add 12" (30.5 cm). Divide the measurement by 40" (101.5 cm) to calculate the number of strips needed. Cut 2¼" (5.7 cm) wide strips from selvage to selvage (crosswise grain). Pin strips, right sides together, at right angles; strips will form a V. Stitch diagonally across strips.

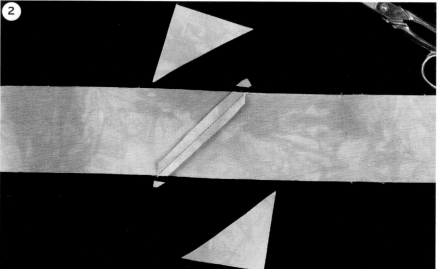

2 Trim seam allowances to ¼" (6 mm). Press seam open. Trim points even edges.

3 Fold binding in half lengthwise, wrong sides together; press. Lay binding along the edge of the quilt top. Leave an 8" tail, stitch the binding in place with about ¼" (6 mm) seam allowance.

How to Bind a Quilt with Double Mitered Binding (cont.)

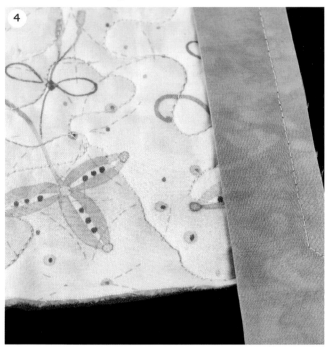

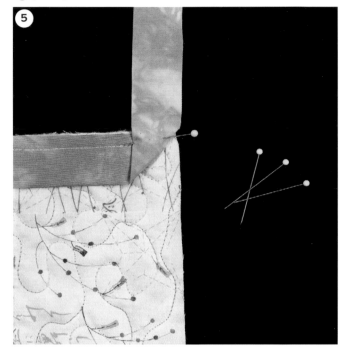

4 Stop sewing ¼" (6 mm) from the corner of the quilt. With needle in down position, pivot quilt top and stitch diagonally to the corner of the quilt. Clip the thread.

5 Fold the binding up and away from the quilt top.

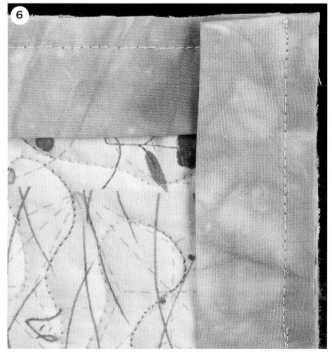

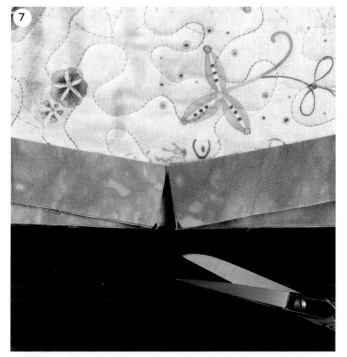

6 Fold the binding back down onto itself; keeping the fold aligned with the edge of the quilt top. Begin stitching from the upper fold, and continue to the next corner. Repeat steps 4 to 6 for the remaining edges.

7 Stop sewing 8" (20.3 cm) from the starting point; remove the quilt from the sewing machine and lay quilt on flat surface. Fold the two tail ends back on themselves so they meet in the middle of the unsewn edge. Clip ⅛" (3 mm) notches into bindings at the meeting point.

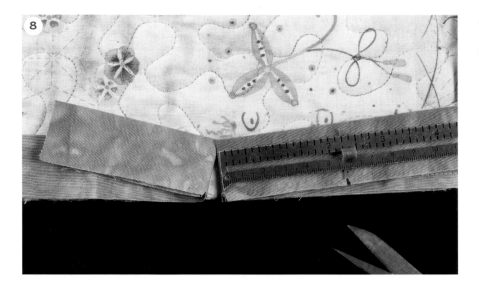

8 On the end tail, measure 2¼" (5.7 cm) from notch and cut a second set of notches.

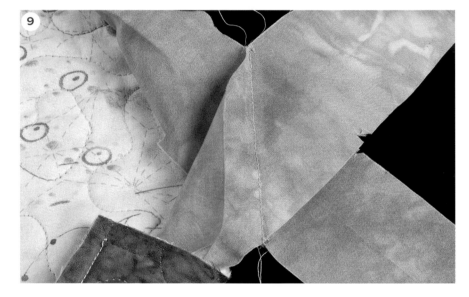

9 Position the quilt to the left, and binding and quilt edge on the right. With your left hand, open the end tail so the right side is facing you. With your right hand, open the start tail with wrong side facing you. Lay the start tail on top of the end tail at a diagonal; right sides together; notches matching on raw edges of binding. Pin in place; mark diagonal line. Sew on marked edge. Finger press the seam open; check for accuracy before trimming seam to ¼" (6 mm).

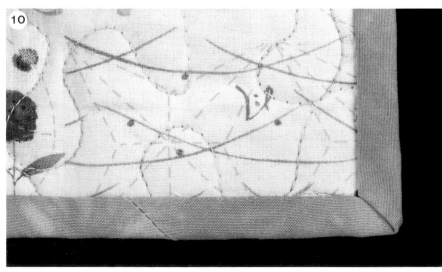

10. Finish stitching the binding to the quilt top. Fold the binding over the raw edges to the back. Blindstich binding in place, with the folded edge covering the line of machine stitching. A miter will form at each corner. Blindstich the mitered corner in place.